Tales of Cornish
Mariners and Mermaids

Robert Hunt

Bossiney Books • Exeter

Robert Hunt

Robert Hunt (1807-1887) was a scientist and poet, born in Devonport. His father was a naval officer who drowned while Robert was still a child. He studied as a chemist in London, but became ill in 1828, and moved back to convalesce in Cornwall, where he gathered folk-lore tales.

In 1840 he was appointed secretary to the Royal Cornwall Polytechnic Society in Falmouth, then became keeper of mining records at the Museum of Economic Geology in London, where he also lectured.

At the same time he was an early pioneer of photography, publishing a *Manual of Photography* in 1841, and wrote poetry.

In 1865 he published *Popular Romances of the West of England or the drolls, traditions and superstitions of old Cornwall*, drawing on his own research and that of Thomas Quiller Couch and William Bottrell. The present book is entirely taken from this source. Minor editorial changes have been made, in particular to place-name spellings.

This repint 2024
First published 2021 by Bossiney Books Ltd,
68 Thorndale Courts, Whitycombe Way, Exeter, Devon, EX4 2NY
www.bossineybooks.com

ISBN 978-1-915664-40-2

Acknowledgements

The illustration on page 38 is by Tony Morris.

Printed in Great Britain by Short Run Press, Exeter

The pilot's ghost story

I prefer giving this story in the words in which it was communicated. For its singular character, it is a ghost story well worth preserving.

Just seventeen years since, I went down on the wharf from my house one night about twelve and one in the morning, to see whether there was any 'hobble' [hazardous situation], and found a sloop, the *Sally* of St Ives, in the bay, bound for Hayle. [The *Sally* was wrecked at St Ives one Saturday afternoon in the spring of 1862.]

When I got by the White Hart public-house, I saw a man leaning against a post on the wharf. I spoke to him, wished him good morning, and asked him what o'clock it was, but to no purpose. I was not to be easily frightened, for I didn't believe in ghosts; and finding I got no answer to my repeated inquiries, I approached close to him and said, 'Thee'rt a queer sort of fellow, not to speak; I'd speak to the devil, if he were to speak to me. Who art a at all? thee'st needn't think to frighten me. That thee wasn't do, if thou wert twice so ugly; who art a at all?'

He turned his great ugly face on me, glared abroad his great eyes, opened his mouth, and it was a mouth sure nuff. Then I saw pieces of sea-weed and bits of sticks in his whiskers; the flesh of his face and hands were parboiled, just like a woman's hands after a good day's washing. Well, I did not like his looks a bit, and sheered off; but he followed close by my side, and I could hear the water squashing in his shoes every step he took. Well, I stopped a bit, and thought to be a little bit civil to him, and spoke to him again, but no answer.

I then thought I would go to seek for another of our crew, and knock him up to get the vessel, and had got about fifty or sixty yards, when I turned to see if he was following me, but saw him where I left him. Fearing he would come after me, I ran for my life the few steps that I had to go. But when I got to the door, to my horror there stood the man in the door grinning horribly. I shook like as aspen-leaf; my hat lifted from my head; the sweat boiled out of me. What to do I didn't know, and in the house there was such a row, as if everybody was breaking up everything.

After a bit I went in, for the door was 'on the latch,' – that is, not locked – and called the captain of the boat, and got light, but everything was all right, nor had he heard any noise. We went out aboard of the *Sally*, and I put her into Hayle, but I felt ill enough to be in bed.

I left the vessel to come home as soon as I could, but it took me four hours to walk two miles, and I had to lie down in the road, and was carried home to St Ives in a cart as far as the Terrace; from there I was carried home by my brothers, and put to bed. Three days afterwards all my hair fell off as if I had had my head shaved. The roots, and for about half an inch from the roots, being quite white. I was ill six months, and the doctor's bill was £4. 17s. 6d. for attendance and medicine. So you see I have reason to believe in the existence of spirits as much as Mr Wesley had. My hair grew again, and twelve months after I had as good a head of dark-brown hair as ever.

The phantom ship

Years long ago, one night, a gig's crew was called to go off to a hobble, to the westwards of St Ives Head. No sooner was one boat launched than several others were put off from the shore, and a stiff chase was maintained, each one being eager to get to the ship, as she had the appearance of a foreign trader. The hull was clearly visible, she was a schooner-rigged vessel, with a light over her bows.

Away they pulled, and the boat which had been first launched still kept ahead by dint of mechanical power and skill. All the men had thrown off their jackets to row with more freedom. At length the helmsman cried out, 'Stand ready to board her.' The sailor rowing the bow oar slipped it out of the row-lock, and stood on the fore-thwart, taking his jacket on his arm, ready to spring aboard.

The vessel came so close to the boat that they could see the men, and the bow-oar man made a grasp at her bulwarks. His hand found nothing solid, and he fell, being caught by one of his mates, back into the boat, instead of into the water. Then ship and lights disappeared. The next morning the *Neptune* of London, Captain Richard Grant, was wrecked at Gwithian, and all perished. The captain's body was picked up after a few days, and that of his son also. They were both buried in Gwithian churchyard.

Jack Harry's lights

The phantom lights are called, they tell me, 'Jack Harry's lights', because he was the first man who was fooled by them. They are generally observed before a gale, and the ship seen is like the ship which is sure to be wrecked. The man who communicated this to me said, 'What or how it is we can't tell, but the fact of its being seen is too plain.'

The following is another version, which I received from an old pilot.

Some five years ago, on a Sunday night, the wind being strong, our crew heard of a large vessel in the offing, after we came out of chapel. We manned our big boat, the *Ark* – she was nearly new then – and away we went, under close-reefed foresail and little mizen, the sea going over us at a sweet rate. The vessel stood just off the head, the wind blowing WNW. We had gone off four or five miles, and we thought we were up alongside, when, lo! she slipped to windward a league or more. Well, off we went after her, and a good beating match we had, too; but the *Ark* was a safe craft, and we neared and neared till, as we thought, we got up close. Away she whizzed in a minute, in along to Godrevy, just over the course we sailed; so we gave it up for Jack Harry's light, and, with wet jackets and disappointed hopes, we bore up for the harbour, prepared to hear of squalls, which came heavier than ever next day.

Scores of pilots have seen and been led a nice chase after them. They are just the same as the *Flying Dutchman*, seen off the Cape of Good Hope.

Another man informed me that, once coming down channel, they had a phantom ship alongside of them for miles: it was a moonlit night, with a thin rain and mist. They could see several men aboard moving about. They hailed her several times, but could not get an answer, 'and we didn't know what to think of her, when all at once she vanished.'

The pirate wrecker and the death ship

One lovely evening in the autumn, a strange ship was seen at a short distance from Cape Cornwall. The little wind there was blew from the land, but she did not avail herself of it. She was evidently permitted to drift with the tide, which was flowing southward, and curving in round Whitesand Bay towards the Land's End. The vessel, from her peculiar rig, created no small amount of alarm amongst the fishermen, since it told them that she was manned by pirates; and a large body of men and women watched her movements from behind the rocks at Caragloose. At length, when within a couple of pistol-shots off the shore, a boat was lowered and manned. Then a man, whose limited movements showed him to be heavily ironed, was brought to the side of the ship and evidently forced – for several pistols were held at his head – into the boat, which then rowed rapidly to the shore in Priest's Cove. The waves of the Atlantic Ocean fell so gently on the strand, that there was no difficulty in beaching the boat. The prisoner was made to stand up, and his ponderous chains were removed from his arms and ankles. In a frenzy of passion he attacked the sailors, but they were too many and too strong for him, and the fight terminated by his being thrown into the water, and left to scramble up on the dry sands. They pushed the boat off with a wild shout, and this man stood uttering fearful imprecations on his former comrades.

It subsequently became known that this man was so monstrously wicked that even the pirates would no longer endure him, and hence they had recourse to this means of ridding themselves of him. It is not necessary to tell how this wretch settled himself at Tregaseal, and lived by a system of wrecking, pursued with unheard-of cruelties and cunning. 'It's too frightful to tell,' says my correspondent, 'what was said about his doings. We scarcely believed half of the vile things we heard, till we saw what took place at his death. But one can't say he died, because he was taken off bodily. We shall never know the scores, perhaps hundreds, of ships that old sinner has brought on the cliffs, by fastening his lantern to the neck of his horse, with its head tied close to the forefoot. The horse, when driven along the cliff, would, by its motion, cause the lantern to be taken for the stern-light of a ship; then the vessel would come right in on the rocks, since those on board would expect to find plenty of sea-room; and, if any of the poor sailors escaped a watery grave, the old wretch would give them a worse death, by knocking them on the head with his hatchet, or cutting off their hands as they tried to grasp the ledges of the rocks.'

A life of extreme wickedness was at length closed with circumstances of unusual terror – so terrible that the story is told with feelings of awe even at the present day. The old wretch fought lustily with death, but at length the time of his departure came. It was in the time of the barley-harvest. Two men were in a field on the cliff, a little below the house, mowing. A universal calm prevailed, and there was not a breath of wind to stir the corn. Suddenly a breeze passed by them, and they heard the words, 'The time is come, but the man isn't come.' These words appeared to float in the breeze from the sea, and consequently it attracted their attention. Looking out to sea, they saw a black, heavy, square-rigged ship, with all her sails set, coming in against wind and tide, and not a hand to be seen on board. The sky became black as night around the ship, and as she came under the cliff – and she came so close that the top of the masts could scarcely be perceived – the darkness resolved itself into a lurid storm-cloud, which extended high into the air. The sun shone brilliantly over the country, except on the house of the pirate at Tregaseal – that was wrapt in the deep shadow of the cloud.

The men, in terror, left their work; they found all the neighbours gathered around the door of the pirate's cottage, none of them daring to enter it. Parson —— had been sent for by the terrified peasants, this divine being celebrated for his power of driving away evil spirits.

The dying wrecker was in a state of agony, crying out, in tones of the most intense terror, 'The devil is tearing at me with nails like the claws of a hawk! Put out the sailors with their bloody hands!' and using, in the paroxysms of pain, the most profane imprecations. The parson, the doctor, and two of the bravest of the fishermen, were the only persons in the room. They related that at one moment the room was as dark as the grave, and that at the next it was so light that every hair on the old man's head could be seen standing on end. The parson used all his influence to dispel the evil spirit. His powers were so potent that he reduced the devil to the size of a fly, but he could not put him out of the room. All this time the room appeared as if filled with the sea, with the waves surging violently to and fro, and one could hear the breakers roaring, as if standing on the edge of the cliff in a storm. At last there was a fearful crash of thunder, and a blaze of the intensest lightning. The house appeared on fire, and the ground shook, as if with an earthquake. All rushed in terror from the house, leaving the dying man to his fate.

The storm raged with fearful violence, but appeared to contract its dimensions. The black cloud, which was first seen to come in with the black ship, was moving, with a violent internal motion, over the wrecker's house. The cloud rolled together, smaller and smaller, and suddenly, with the blast of a whirlwind, it passed from Tregaseal to the ship, and she was impelled, amidst the flashes of lightning and roarings of thunder, away over the sea.

The dead body of the pirate-wrecker lay a ghastly spectacle, with eyes expanded and the mouth partly open, still retaining the aspect of his last mortal terror. As every one hated him, they all desired to remove his corpse as rapidly as possible from the sight of man. A rude coffin was rapidly prepared, and the body was carefully cased in its boards. They tell me the coffin was carried to the churchyard, but that it was too light to have contained the body, and that it was followed by a black pig, which joined the company forming the procession, nobody knew where, and disappeared nobody knew when. When they reached the church stile, a storm, similar in its character to that which heralded the wrecker's death, came on.

The bearers of the coffin were obliged to leave it outside the churchyard stile and rush into the church for safety. The storm lasted long and raged with violence, and all was as dark as night. A sudden blaze of light, more vivid than before, was seen, and those who had the hardihood to look out saw that the lightning had set fire to the coffin, and it was being borne away through the air, blazing and whirling wildly in the grasp of such a whirlwind as no man ever witnessed before or since.

The spectre ship of Porthcurno

Porthcurno Cove is situated a little to the west of the Logan Stone. There, as in nearly all the coves around the coast, once existed a small chapel or oratory, which appears to have been dedicated to St Levan. There exists now a little square enclosure about the size of a *bougie* [sheep's house] which is all that remains of this little holy place. Looking up the valley, you may see a few trees, with the chimney-tops and part of the roof of an old-fashioned house. That place is Raftra, where they say St Levan Church was to have been built; but as fast as the stones were taken there by day, they were removed by night to the place of the present church. (These performances are usually the act of the devil, but I have no information as to the saint or sinner who did this work.) Raftra House, at the time it was built, was the largest mansion west of Penzance. It is said to have been erected by the Tresillians, and, ere it was finished, they appear to have been obliged to sell house and lands for less than it had cost them to build the house.

This valley is in every respect a melancholy spot, and during a period of storms, or at night, it is exactly the place which might well be haunted by demon revellers. In the days of the saint from whom the parish has its name – St Levan – he lived a long way up from the cove, at a place called Bodellan, and his influence made that, which is now so dreary, a garden. By his pure holiness he made the wilderness a garden of flowers, and spread gladness where now is desolation.

Few persons cared to cross that valley after nightfall; and it is not more than thirty years since that I had a narrative from an inhabitant of Penberth, that he himself had seen the spectre ship sailing over the land.

This strange apparition is said to have been observed frequently, coming in from sea about nightfall, when the mists were rising from the marshy ground in the Bottoms.

Onward came the ill-omened craft. It passed steadily through the breakers on the shore, glided up over the sands, and steadily pursued its course over the dry land, as if it had been water. She is described to have been a black, square-rigged, single-masted affair, usually, but not always, followed by a boat. No crew was ever seen. It is supposed they were below, and that the hatches were battened down. On it went to Bodellan, where St Levan formerly dwelt. It would then steer its course to Chegwidden, and there vanish like smoke.

Many of the old people have seen this ship, and no one ever saw it upon whom some bad luck was not sure to fall.

This ship is somehow connected with a strange man who returned from sea and went to live at Chegwidden. It may be five hundred years since – it may be but fifty.

He was accompanied by a servant of foreign and forbidding aspect, who continued to be his only attendant; and this servant was never known to speak to any one save his master. It is said by some they were pirates; others make them more familiar, by calling them privateers; while some insist upon it they were American buccaneers.

Whatever they may have been, there was but little seen of them by any of their neighbours. They kept a boat at Porthcurno Cove, and at daylight they would start for sea, never returning until night, and not unfrequently remaining out the whole of the night, especially if the weather was tempestuous. This kind of sea-life was varied by hunting. It mattered not to them whether it was day or night; when the storm was loudest, there was this strange man, accompanied either by his servant or by the devil, and the midnight cry of his dogs would disturb the country.

This mysterious being died, and then the servant sought the aid of a few of the peasantry to bear his coffin to the churchyard. The corpse was laid in the grave, around which the dogs were gathered, with the foreigner in their midst. As soon as the earth was thrown on the coffin, man and dogs disappeared, and, strange to say, the boat disappeared at the same moment from the cove. It has never since been seen; and from that day to this no one has been able to keep a boat in Porthcurno Cove.

The lady with the lantern

The night was dark and the wind high. The heavy waves rolled round the point of the Island into St Ives Bay, as Atlantic waves only can roll. Everything bespoke a storm of no ordinary character. There were no ships in the bay – not a fishing-boat was afloat. The few small trading vessels had run into Hayle for shelter, or had nestled themselves within that very unquiet resting-place, St Ives pier. The fishing-boats were all high and dry on the sands.

Moving over the rocks which run out into the sea from the eastern side of the Island, was seen a light. It passed over the most rugged ridges, formed by the intrusive Greenstone masses, and over the sharp edges of the upturned slate-rocks, with apparent ease. Forth and back – to and from – wandered the light.

'Ha!' said an old sailor with a sigh, as he looked out over the sea; 'a sad night! a sad night! The Lady and the Lantern is out.'

'The Lady and the Lantern,' repeated I, 'what do you mean?'

'The light out yonder – '

'Is from the lantern of some fisherman looking for something he has lost,' interrupted I.

'Never a fisherman nor a salt either would venture there to-night,' said the sailor.

'What is it, then?' I curiously inquired.

'Ha'ast never heard of the Lady and the Lantern?' asked a woman who was standing by.

'Never.'

Without any preface, she began at once to enlighten me. I am compelled, however, to reduce her rambling story to something like order, and to make her long-drawn tale as concise as possible.

In the year — there were many wrecks around the coast. It was a melancholy time. For more than a month there had been a succession of storms, each one more severe than the preceding one. At length, one evening, just about dusk, a large ship came suddenly out of the mist. Her position, it was at once discovered, equally by those on board and by the people on the shore, was perilous beyond hope. The sailors, as soon as they saw how near they were to the shore, made every effort to save the ship, and then to prepare for saving themselves. The tempest raged with such fury from the west, that the ship parted her anchors at the moment her strain came upon them, and she swang round – her only sail flying into ribbons in the gale – rushing, as it were, eagerly upon her fate. Presently she struck violently upon a sunken rock, and her masts went by the board, the waves sweeping over her, and clearing her decks. Many perished at once, and, as each successive wave urged her onward, others of the hardy and daring seamen were swept into the angry sea.

Notwithstanding the severity of the storm, a boat was manned by the St Ives fishermen, and launched from within the pier. Their perfect knowledge of their work enabled them, by the efforts of willing hearts, anxiously desiring to succour the distressed, to round the pier-head, and to row towards the ship.

These fishermen brought their boat near to the ship. It was impossible to get close to her, and they called to the sailors on board to throw them ropes. This they were enabled to do, and some two or three of the sailors lowered themselves by their aid, and were hauled into the boat.

Then a group appeared on the deck, surrounding and supporting a lady, who held a child in her arms. They were imploring her to give her charge into the strong arms of a man ere they endeavoured to pass her from the ship to the boat.

The lady could not be prevailed on to part with the infant. The ship was fast breaking up, not a moment could be lost. So the lady, holding her child, was lowered into the sea, and eagerly the fishermen drew her through the waves towards the boat.

In her passage the lady had fainted, and she was taken into the boat without the infant. The child had fallen from her arms, and was lost in the boiling waters.

Many of the crew were saved by these adventurous men, and taken safely into St Ives. Before morning the shore was strewed with fragments of wreck, and the mighty ship had disappeared.

Life returned to the lady; but, finding that her child was gone, it returned without hope, and she speedily closed her eyes in death. In the churchyard they buried her; but, shortly after her burial, a lady was seen to pass over the wall of the churchyard, on to the beach, and walk towards the Island. There she spent hours amidst the rocks, looking for her child, and not finding it, she would sigh deeply and return to her grave. When the nights were tempestuous or very dark, she carried a lantern; but on fine nights she made her search without a light. The Lady and the Lantern have ever been regarded as predictors of disaster on this shore.

The bells of Forrabury church

To this day the tower of Forrabury Church, or, as it is called by Mr Hawker, 'the silent tower of Bottreaux,' remains without bells. At Forrabury the chimes have never sounded for a marriage, the knell has never been heard for a funeral.

In days long ago, the inhabitants of the parish of Forrabury which does not cover a square mile, but which now includes the chief part of the town of Boscastle and its harbour, resolved to have a peal of bells which should rival those of the neighbouring church of Tintagel, which are said to have rung merrily at the marriage, and tolled solemnly at the death, of Arthur.

The bells were cast; the bells were blessed; and the bells were shipped for Forrabury. Few voyages were more favourable; and the ship glided, with a fair wind, along the northern shores of Cornwall, waiting for the tide to carry her safely into the harbour of Bottreaux.

The vesper bells rang out at Tintagel; and the pilot, when he heard the blessed sound, devoutly crossed himself, and bending his knee, thanked God for the safe and quick voyage which they had made.

The captain laughed at the superstition of the pilot, as he called it, and swore that they had only to thank themselves for the speedy voyage, and that, with his arm at the helm, and his judgment to guide them, they should soon have a happy landing. The pilot checked this profane speech; but the wicked captain – and he swore more impiously than ever that all was due to himself and his men – laughed to scorn the pilot's prayer.

'May God forgive you!' was the pilot's reply.

Those who are familiar with the northern shores of Cornwall will know that sometimes a huge wave, generated by some mysterious power in the wide Atlantic, will roll on, overpowering everything by its weight and force.

While yet the captain's oaths were heard, and while the inhabitants

on the shore were looking out from the cliffs, expecting, within an hour, to see the vessel, charged with their bells, safe in their harbour, one of these vast swellings of the ocean was seen. Onward came the grand billow in all the terror of its might. The ship rose not upon the waters as it came onward. She was overwhelmed, and sank in an instant, close to the land.

As the vessel sank, the bells were heard tolling with a muffled sound, as if ringing the death-knell of the ship and sailors, of whom the good pilot alone escaped with life.

When storms are coming, and only then, the bells of Forrabury, with their dull, muffled sound, are heard from beneath the heaving sea, a warning to the wicked; and the tower has remained to this day silent.

The drowned 'hailing their names'

The fishermen dread to walk at night near those parts of the shore where there may have been wrecks. The souls of the drowned sailors appear to haunt those spots, and the 'calling of the dead' has frequently been heard. I have been told that, under certain circumstances, especially before the coming of storms, or at certain seasons, but always at night, these callings are common. Many a fisherman has declared he has heard the voices of dead sailors 'hailing their own names'.

The voice from the sea

A fisherman or a pilot was walking one night on the sands at Porth-Towan, when all was still save the monotonous fall of the light waves upon the sand. He distinctly heard a voice from the sea exclaiming:

'The hour is come, but not the man.'

This was repeated three times when a black figure, like that of a man, appeared on the top of the hill. It paused for a moment, then rushed impetuously down the steep incline, over the sands, and was lost in the sea. In different forms this story is told all around the Cornish coast.

The smuggler's token

Until about the time of the close of the last French war, a large portion of the inhabitants of the south-west coast of Cornwall were in some way or other connected with the practice of smuggling. The traffic with the opposite coast was carried on principally in boats or undecked vessels. The risks encountered by their crews produced a race of hardy, fearless men, a few of whom are still living, and it has been said that the Government of those days winked at the infraction of the law, from an unwillingness to destroy so excellent a school for seamen. Recently the demand for ardent spirits has so fallen off that there is no longer an inducement to smuggle; still it is sometimes exultingly rumoured that, the 'Coast Guard having been cleverly put off the scent, a cargo has been successfully run.'

The little coves in the Lizard promontory formed the principal trading places, the goods being taken as soon as landed to various places of concealment, whence they were withdrawn as required for disposal. About eighty years since, a boat, laden with 'ankers' of spirits, was about, with its crew, to leave Mullion Cove for Newlyn. One of the farmers concerned in the venture, members of whose family are still living, was persuaded to accompany them, and entered the boat for the purpose, but, recollecting he had business at Helston, got out again, and the boat left without him. On his return from Helston, late in the evening, he sat down, exclaiming, 'The boat and all on board are lost! I met the men as I passed the top of Halzephron (a very high cliff on the road) with their hair and clothes dripping wet!'

In spite of the arguments of his friends, he persisted in his statement. The boat and crew were never more heard of, and the farmer was so affected by the circumstance, that he pined and died shortly after.

The Hooper, or Hooter, of Sennen Cove

This was supposed to be a spirit which took the form of a band of misty vapour, stretching across the bay, so opaque that nothing could be seen through it. It was regarded as a kindly interposition of some ministering spirit, to warn the fishermen against venturing to sea. This appearance was always followed, and often suddenly, by a severe storm. It is seldom or ever seen now. One profane old fisherman would not be warned by the bank of fog. The weather was fine on the shore, and the waves fell tranquilly on the sands; and this aged sinner, declaring he would not be made a fool of, persuaded some young men to join him. They manned a boat, and the aged leader, having with him a threshing-flail, blasphemously declared that he would drive the spirit away; and he vigorously beat the fog with the 'threshel' – so the flail is called.

The boat passed through the fog, and went to sea. A severe storm came on. No one ever saw the boat or the men again; and since that time the Hooper has been rarely seen.

How to eat pilchards

It is unlucky to commence eating pilchards, or, indeed, any kind of fish, from the head downwards. I have often heard persons rebuked for committing such a grievous sin, which is 'sure to turn the heads of the fish away from the coasts'.

The legitimate process – mark this, all fish-eaters – is to eat the fish from the tail towards the head. This brings the fish to our shores, and secures good luck to the fishermen.

Pilchards crying for more

When there is a large catch of fish (pilchards) they are preserved – put in bulk, as the phrase is – by being rubbed with salt, and placed in regular order, one on the other, head and tails alternately, forming regular walls of fish.

The fish often, when so placed, make a squeaking noise; this is called 'crying for more' and is regarded as a most favourable sign. More fish may soon be expected to be brought to the same cellar.

The noise which is heard is really produced by the bursting of the air-bladders; when many break together, which, when hundreds of thousands are piled in a mass, is not unusual, the sound is a loud one.

The pressing stones

Those who are not familiar with the process of 'curing' (salting) pilchards for the Italian markets, will require a little explanation to understand the accompanying story.

The pilchards being caught in vast quantities, often, amounting to many thousand hogsheads at a time, in an enclosing net called a 'seine', are taken out of it – the larger net – in a smaller net called the 'tuck net', and from it loaded into boats and taken to the shore. They are quickly transferred to the fish-cellars, and 'put in bulk' – that is, they are well rubbed with salt, and carefully packed up – all interstitial spaces being filled with salt – in a pile several feet in height and depth. They remain in this condition for about six weeks, when they are removed from 'the bulk', washed, and put into barrels in very regular order. The barrels being filled with pilchards, pressing-stones – round masses of granite, weighing about a hundredweight – with an iron hook fixed into them for the convenience of moving, are placed on the fish. By this they are much compressed, and a considerable quantity of oil is squeezed out of them. This process being completed, the cask is 'headed', marked, and is ready for exportation.

Jem Tregose and his old woman, with two sons and a daughter, lived over one of the fish-cellars in St Ives. For many years there had been a great scarcity of fish; their cellar had been empty; Jem and his boys were fishermen, and it had long been hard times with them. It is true they went out 'hook-and-line' fishing now and then, and got a little money. They had gone over to Ireland on the herring-fishing, but very little luck attended them.

Summer had passed away, and the early autumn was upon them. The seine-boats were out day after day, but no 'signs of fish'. One evening, when the boys came home, Ann Jenny Tregose had an unusual smile upon her face, and her daughter Janniper, who had long suffered from the 'megrims', was in capital spirits.

'Well, mother,' says one of the sons, 'and what ails thee a'?'

'The press-stones a bin rolling.'

'Haas they, sure enuff,' says the old man.

'Ees! ees!' exclaims Janniper; 'they has been making a skimmage!'

'Hark ye,' cries the old woman, 'there they go again.'

And sure enough there was a heavy rolling of the stones in the cellar below them. It did not require much imagination to imagine these round granite pebbles sliding themselves down on the 'couse', or stone flooring, and dividing themselves up into sets, as if for a dance – a regular 'cows' courant', or game of romps.

'Fish to-morrow!' exclaimed the old woman. The ejaculations of each one of the party shewed their perfect faith in the belief, that the stones rolling down from the heap, in which they had been useless for some time, was a certain indication that pilchards were approaching the coast.

Early on the morrow the old man and his sons were on their 'stem' and shortly after daylight the cry of 'Heva! heva!' was heard from the hills; the seine was shot, and ere night a large quantity of fish might be seen in the cellar, and every one joyous.

Merrymaids and merrymen

The 'merry-maids' of the Cornish fishermen and sailors possess the well-recognised features of the mermaid. The Breton ballad, quoted by Mr Keightley, relating to the Morgan (sea-women) and the Morverch (sea-daughters), peculiarly adapts itself to the Cornish merry-maid.

> 'Fisher, hast thou seen the mermaid combing her hair, yellow as gold, by the noontide sun, at the edge of the water?'
> 'I have seen the fair mermaid; I have also heard her singing her songs plaintive as the waves.'

The Irish legends make us acquainted with the amours of men with those sea-sirens. We learn that the Merrows, or Moruachs, came occasionally from the sea, and interested themselves in the affairs of man. Amongst the fragments which have been gathered, here a pebble and there a pebble, along the Western coast, will be found similar narratives.

The sirens of the Aegean Sea – probably the parents of the mediaeval mermaid – possess in a pre-eminent degree the beauty and the falsehood of all the race. Like all other things, even those mythical creations take colour from that they work in, like the dyer's hand. The Italian mermaid is the true creature of the romance of the sunny South; while the lady of our own southern seas, although she possesses much in common with her Mediterranean sister, has less poetry, but more human sympathy. The following stories, read in connection with those given by Mr Keightley and by Mr Croker, will show this.

[Thomas Keightley (1789-1872), an Irish folklorist, wrote *The Fairy Mythology*, published in 1828. Thomas Crofton Croker (1798-1854) wrote *Fairy Legends and Traditions of the South of Ireland*, published in 1825.]

When, five-and-thirty years since, I spent several nights in a fisherman's cottage on a south-western coast, I was treated to many a long yarn respecting mermaids seen by the father and his sons in the southern ocean. The appearance of those creatures on our own shores, they said, was rare; but still they knew they had been seen. From them I learned of more than one family who have received mysterious powers from the sea-nymphs; and I have since heard that members of those families still live, and that they intimate to their credulous friends their firm belief that this power, which they say has been transmitted to them, was derived, by some one of their ancestors, from merman or mermaiden.

Usually those creatures are associated with some catastrophe; but they are now and then spoken of as the benefactors of man.

One word more. The story of 'The Mermaid's Vengeance' has been produced from three versions of evidently the same legend, which differed in many respects one from the other, yet agreeing in the main with each other. The first I heard at the Lizard, or rather at Coverack; the second in Sennen Cove, near the Land's End; the third at Perranzabuloe. I have preferred the last locality, as being peculiarly fitted for the home of a mermaid story, and because the old man who told the tale there was far more graphic in his incidents; and these were strung more closely together than either of the other stories.

The mermaid of Padstow

The port of Padstow has a good natural harbour, so far as a rocky area goes, but it is so choked up with drifting sands as to be nearly useless. A peasant recently thus explained the cause. He told how 'it was once deep water for the largest vessel, and under the care of a merry-maid as he called her; but one day, as she was sporting on the surface, a fellow with a gun shot at her.' She dived for a moment but, re-appearing, raised her right arm, and vowed that henceforth the harbour should be desolate. 'And,' added the old man, 'it always will be so.'

We have had commissions, and I know not what, about converting this place into a harbour of refuge. A harbour of refuge would be a great blessing, but not all the Government commissions in the world could keep the sand out, or make the harbour deep enough to swim a frigate, unless the parsons can find out the way to take up the merry-maid's curse.

The Mermaid's Rock

To the westward of the beautiful Cove of Lamorna is a rock which has through all time borne the above name. I have never been able to learn any special story in connection with this rock. There exists the popular fancy of a lady showing herself here previous to a storm with, of course, the invariable comb and glass. She is said to have been heard singing most plaintively before a wreck, and that, all along the shore, the spirits have echoed her in low moaning voices. Young men are said to have swum off to the rock, lured by the songs which they heard, but they have never returned. Have we not in this a dim shadow of the story of the Sirens?

The mermaid of Seaton

Near Looe, that is, between Downderry and Looe, there is a little sand-beach called Seaton. Tradition tells us that here once stood a goodly commercial town bearing this name, and that when it was in its pride, Plymouth was but a small fishing-village.

The town of Seaton is said to have been overwhelmed with sand at an early period, the catastrophe having been brought about, as in the case of the filling up of Padstow harbour, by the curse of a mermaid, who had suffered some injury from the sailors belonging to this port. Beyond this I have been unable to glean any story worth preserving.

The old man of Cury

More than a hundred years since, on a fine summer day, when the sun shone brilliantly from a cloudless sky, an old man from the parish of Cury, or, as it was called in olden time, Corantyn, was walking on the sands in one of the coves near the Lizard Point. The old man was meditating, or at least he was walking onward, either thinking deeply, or not thinking at all that is, he was 'lost in thought' when suddenly he came upon a rock on which was sitting a beautiful girl with fair hair, so long that it covered her entire person. On the in-shore side of the rock was a pool of the most transparent water, which had been left by the receding tide in the sandy hollow the waters had scooped out. This young creature was so absorbed in her occupation, arranging her hair in the watery mirror, or in admiration of her own lovely face, that she was unconscious of an intruder.

The old man stood looking at her for some time ere he made up his mind how to act. At length he resolved to speak to the maiden. 'What cheer, young one?' he said; 'what art thee doing there by thyself, then, this time o' day?' As soon as she heard the voice, she slid off the rock entirely under the water.

The old man could not tell what to make of it. He thought the girl would drown herself, so he ran on to the rock to render her assistance, conceiving that in her fright at being found naked by a man she had fallen into the pool, and possibly it was deep enough to drown her. He looked into the water, and, sure enough, he could make out the head and shoulders of a woman, and long hair floating like fine sea-weeds all over the pond, hiding what appeared to him to be a fish's tail. He could not, however, see anything distinctly, owing to the abundance of hair floating around the figure. The old man had heard of mermaids from the fishermen of Gunwalloe; so he conceived this lady must be one, and he was at first very much frightened. He saw that the young lady was quite as much terrified as he was, and that, from shame or fear, she endeavoured to hide herself in the crevices of the rock, and bury herself under the sea-weeds.

Summoning courage, at last the old man addressed her, 'Don't 'e be afraid, my dear. You needn't mind me. I wouldn't do ye any harm. I'm an old man, and wouldn't hurt ye any more than your grandfather.'

After he had talked in this soothing strain for some time, the young lady took courage, and raised her head above the water. She was crying bitterly, and, as soon as she could speak, she begged the old man to go away.

'I must know, my dearie, something about ye, now I have caught ye. It is not every day that an old man catches a merry-maid, and I have heard some strange tales of you water-ladies. Now, my dear, don't 'e be afraid, I would not hurt a single hair of that beautiful head. How came ye here?

After some further coaxing she told the old man the following story: she and her husband and little ones had been busy at sea all the morning, and they were very tired with swimming in the hot sun; so the merman proposed that they should retire to a cavern, which they were in the habit of visiting in Kynance Cove. Away they all swam, and entered the cavern at mid-tide. As there was some nice soft weed, and the cave was deliciously cool, the merman was disposed to sleep, and told them not to wake him until the rise of the tide. He was soon fast asleep, snoring most lustily.

The children crept out and were playing on the lovely sands; so the mermaid thought she should like to look at the world a little. She looked with delight on the children rolling to and fro in the shallow waves, and she laughed heartily at the crabs fighting in their own funny way. 'The scent from the flowers came down over the cliffs so sweetly,' said she, 'that I longed to get nearer the lovely things which yielded those rich odours, and I floated on from rock to rock until I came to this one; and finding that I could not proceed any further, I thought I would seize the opportunity of dressing my hair.' She passed her fingers through those beautiful locks, and shook out a number of small crabs, and much broken sea-weed. She went on to say that she had sat on the rock amusing herself, until the voice of a mortal terrified her, and until then she had no idea that the sea was so far out, and a long dry bar of sand between her and it.

'What shall I do? what shall I do? Oh! I'd give the world to get out to sea! Oh! oh! what shall I do?'

The old man endeavoured to console her; but his attempts were in vain. She told him her husband would 'carry on' most dreadfully if he awoke and found her absent, and he would be certain of awaking at the turn of the tide, as that was his dinner-time. He was very savage when he was hungry, and would as soon eat the children as not, if there was no other food at hand. He was also dreadfully jealous, and if she was not at his side when he awoke, he would at once suspect her of having run off with some other merman. She begged the old man to bear her out to sea. If he would but do so, she would procure him any three things he would wish for. Her entreaties at length prevailed; and, according to her desire, the old man knelt down on the rock with his back towards her. She clasped her fair arms around his neck, and locked her long finny fingers together on his throat. He got up from the rock with his burthen, and carried the mermaid thus across the sands. As she rode in this way, she asked the old man to tell her what he desired.

'I will not wish,' said he, 'for silver and gold, but give me the power to do good to my neighbours: first, to break the spells of witchcraft; next, to charm away diseases; and thirdly, to discover thieves, and restore stolen goods.'

All this she promised he should possess; but he must come to a half-tide rock on another day, and she would instruct him how to accomplish the three things he desired. They had reached the water, and taking her comb from her hair, she gave it to the old man, telling him he had but to comb the water and call her at any time, and she would come to him. The mermaid loosened her grasp, and sliding off the old man's back into the sea, she waved him a kiss and disappeared. At the appointed time the old man was at the half-tide rock, known to the present time as the Mermaid's Rock, and duly he was instructed in many mysteries. Amongst others, he learned to break the spells of witches from man or beast; to prepare a vessel of water, in which to show to any one who had property stolen the face of the thief; to charm shingles, tetters, St Antony's fire and St Vitus's dance; and he learnt also all the mysteries of bramble leaves, and the like.

The mermaid had a woman's curiosity, and she persuaded her old friend to take her to some secret place, from which she could see more of the dry land, and of the funny people who lived on it, 'and had their tails split, so that they could walk'. On taking the mermaid back to the sea, she wished her friend to visit her abode, and promised even to make him young if he would do so, which favour the old gentleman respectfully declined.

A family, well known in Cornwall, have for some generations exercised the power of charming, etc. They account for the possession of this power in the manner related. Some remote great-grandfather was the individual who received the mermaid's comb, which they retain to the present day, and show us evidence of the truth of their being supernaturally endowed. Some people are unbelieving enough to say the comb is only a part of a shark's jaw. Sceptical people are never lovable people.

The mermaid's vengeance

In one of the deep valleys of the parish of Perranzabuloe, which are remarkable for their fertility, and especially for the abundance of fruit which the orchards produce, lived in days long ago, amidst a rudely civilised people, a farmer's labourer and his wife, with one child, a daughter. The man and woman were equally industrious. The neatly white-washed walls of their mud-built cottage, the well-kept gravelled paths, and carefully-weeded beds of their small garden, in which flowers were cultivated for ornament, and vegetables for use, proclaimed at once the character of the inmates. In contrast with the neighbouring cottages, this one, although smaller than many others, had a superior aspect, and the occupiers of it exhibited a strong contrast to those peasants and miners amidst whom they dwelt.

Pennaluna, as the man was called, or Penna the Proud, as he was, in no very friendly spirit, named by his less thoughtful and more impulsive fellows, was, as we have said, a farmer's labourer.

His master was a wealthy yeoman, and he, after many years' experience, was so convinced of the exceeding industry and sterling honesty of Penna, that he made him the manager of an outlying farm in this parish, under the hind (or hine – the Saxon pronunciation is still retained in the West of England), or general supervisor of this and numerous other extensive farms.

Penna was too great a favourite with the Squire to be a favourite of the hind's; he was evidently jealous of him, and from not being himself a man of very strict principles, he hated the unobtrusive goodness of his underling, and was constantly on the watch to discover some cause of complaint. It was not, however, often that he was successful in this. Every task committed to the care of Penna, and he was often purposely overtasked, was executed with great care and despatch.

With the wife of Penna, however, the case was unfortunately different. Honour Penna was as industrious as her husband, and to him she was in all respects a helpmate. She had, however, naturally a proud spirit, and this had been encouraged in her youth by her parents.

Honour was very pretty as a girl, and, indeed, she retained much beauty as a woman. The only education she received was the wild one of experience, and this within a very narrow circle. She grew an ignorant girl, amongst ignorant men and women, few of them being able to write their names, and scarcely any of them to read. There was much native grace about her, and she was flattered by the young men, and envied by the young women of the village, the envy and the flattery being equally pleasant to her. In the same village was born, and brought up, Tom Chenalls, who had, in the course of years, become hind to the Squire. Tom, as a young man, had often expressed himself fond of Honour, but he was always distasteful to the village maiden, and eventually, while yet young, she was married to Pennaluna, who came from the southern coast, bringing with him the recommendation of being a stranger, and an exceedingly hard-working man, who was certain to earn bread, and something more, for his wife and family. In the relations in which these people were now placed towards each other, Chenalls had the opportunity of acting ungenerously towards the Pennas.

The man bore this uncomplainingly, but the woman frequently quarrelled with him whom she felt was an enemy, and whom she still regarded but as her equal. Chenalls was a skilled farmer, and hence was of considerable value to the Squire; but although he was endured for his farming knowledge and his business habits, he was never a favourite with his employer. Penna, on the contrary, was an especial favourite, and the evidences of this were so often brought strikingly under the observation of Chenalls, that it increased the irritation of his hate, for it amounted to that.

For years things went on thus. There was the tranquil suffering of an oppressed spirit manifested in Penna – the angry words and actions of his wife towards the oppressor – and, at the same time, as she with much fondness studied to make their humble home comfortable for her husband, she reviled him not unfrequently for the meek spirit with which he endured his petty, but still trying, wrongs. The hind dared not venture on any positive act of wrong towards those people, yet he lost no chance of annoying them, knowing that the Squire's partiality for Penna would not allow him to venture beyond certain bounds, even in this direction.

Penna's solace was his daughter. She had now reached her

eighteenth year, and with the well-developed form of a woman she united the simplicity of a child. Selina, as she was named, was in many respects beautiful. Her features were regular, and had they been lighted up with more mental fire, they would have been beautiful; but the constant repose, the want of animation, left her face merely a pretty one. Her skin was beautifully white, and transparent to the blue veins which traced their ways beneath it, to the verge of that delicacy which indicates disease; but it did not pass that verge. Selina was full of health, as her well-moulded form at once showed, and her clear blue eye distinctly told. At times there was a lovely tint upon the cheek not the hectic of consumptive beauty, but a pure rosy dye, suffused by the healthy life stream, when it flowed the fastest.

The village gossips, who were always busy with their neighbours, said strange things of this girl. Indeed, it was commonly reported that the real child of the Pennas was a remarkably plain child, in every respect a different being from Selina. The striking difference between the infant and the woman was variously explained by the knowing ones. Two stories were, however, current for miles around the country. One was, that Selina's mother was constantly seen gathering dew in the morning, with which to wash her child, and that the fairies on the Towans had, in pure malice, aided her in giving a temporary beauty to the girl, that it might lead to her betrayal into crime. Why this malice, was never clearly made out.

The other story was, that Honour Penna constantly bathed the child in a certain pool, amidst the arched rocks of Perran, which was a favourite resort of the mermaids; that on one occasion the child, as if in a paroxysm of joy, leapt from her arms into the water, and disappeared. The mother, as may well be supposed, suffered a momentary agony of terror; but presently the babe swam up to the surface of the water, its little face more bright and beautiful than it had ever been before. Great was the mother's joy, and also – as the gossips say – great her surprise at the sudden change in the appearance of her offspring. The mother knew no difference in the child whom she pressed lovingly to her bosom, but all the aged crones in the parish declared it to be a changeling.

This tale lived its day; but, as the girl grew on to womanhood, and showed none of the special qualifications belonging either to fairies or mermaids, it was almost forgotten. The uncomplaining father had solace for all his sufferings in wandering over the beautiful sands with his daughter. Whether it was when the summer seas fell in musical undulations on the shore, or when, stirred by the winter tempests, the great Atlantic waves came up in grandeur, and lashed the resisting sands in giant rage, those two enjoyed the solitude. Hour after hour, from the setting sun time until the clear cold moon flooded the ocean with her smiles of light, would the father and child walk these sands. They seemed never to weary of them and the ocean.

Almost every morning, throughout the milder seasons, Selina was in the habit of bathing, and wild tales were told of the frantic joy with which she would play with the breaking billows. Sometimes floating over, and almost dancing on the crests of the waves, at other times rushing under them, and allowing the breaking waters to beat her to the sands, as though they were loving arms, endeavouring to encircle her form. Certain it is, that Selina greatly enjoyed her bath, but all the rest must be regarded as the creations of the imagination. The most eager to give a construction unfavourable to the simple mortality of the maiden was, however, compelled to acknowledge that there was no evidence in her general conduct to support their surmises. Selina, as an only child, fared the fate of others who are unfortunately so placed, and was, as the phrase is, spoiled. She certainly was allowed to follow her own inclinations without any check. Still her inclinations were bounded to working in the garden, and to leading her father to the sea-shore.

Honour Penna, sometimes, it is true, did complain that Selina could not be trusted with the most ordinary domestic duty. Beyond this, there was one other cause of grief – that was the increasing dislike which Selina exhibited towards entering a church. The girl, notwithstanding constant excuses of being sick, suffering from headache, having a pain in her side, and the like, was often taken by her mother to the church. It is said that she always shuddered as she passed the church-stile, and again on stepping from the porch into the church itself. When once within the house of prayer she evinced no peculiar liking or disliking, observing respectfully all the rules during the performance of the church-service, and generally sleeping, or seeming to sleep, during the sermon. Selina Pennaluna had reached her eighteenth year; she was admired by many of the young men of the parish, but, as if surrounded by a spell, she appeared to keep them all at a distance from her. About this time, a nephew to the Squire, a young soldier, who had been wounded in the wars, came into Cornwall to heal his wounds, and recover health, which had suffered in a trying campaign.

This young man, Walter Trewoofe, was a rare specimen of manhood. Even now, shattered as he was by the combined influences of wounds, an unhealthy climate, and dissipation, he could not but be admired for fineness of form, dignity of carriage, and masculine beauty. It was, however, but too evident, that this young man was his own idol, and that he expected everyone to bow down with him, and worship it. His uncle was proud of Walter, and although the old gentleman could not fail to see many faults, yet he regarded them as the follies of youth, and trusted to their correction with the increase of years and experience. Walter, who was really suffering severely, was ordered by his surgeon, at first, to take short walks on the sea-shore and, as he gained strength, to bathe. He was usually driven in his uncle's pony-carriage to the edge of the sands. Then dismounting he would walk for a short time, and quickly wearying, return in his carriage to the luxuriant couches at the manor-house.

On some of those occasions Walter had observed the father and daughter taking their solitary ramble. He was struck with the quiet beauty of the girl, and seized an early opportunity of stopping Penna to make some general inquiry respecting the bold and beautiful coast. From time to time they thus met, and it would have been evident to any observer that Walter did not so soon weary of the sands as formerly, and that Selina was not displeased with the flattering things he said to her. Although the young soldier had hitherto led a wild life, it would appear as if for a considerable period the presence of goodness had repressed every tendency to evil in his ill-regulated heart. He continued, therefore, for some time playing with his own feelings and those of the childlike being who presented so much of romance, combined with the most homely tameness of character. Selina, it is true, had never yet seen Walter except in the presence of her father, and it is questionable if she had ever for one moment had a warmer feeling than that of the mere pleasure – a silent pride – that a gentleman, at once so handsome, so refined, and the nephew of her father's master, should pay her any attention. Evil eyes were watching with wicked earnestness the growth of passion, and designing hearts were beating quicker with a consciousness that they should eventually rejoice in the downfall of innocence. Tom Chenalls hoped that he might achieve a triumph, if he could but once asperse the character of Selina. He took his measures accordingly. Having noticed the change in the general conduct of his master's nephew, he argued that this was due to the refining influence of a pure mind, acting on one more than ordinarily impressionable to either evil or good.

Walter rapidly recovered health, and with renewed strength the manly energy of his character began to develop itself. He delighted in horse exercise, and Chenalls had always the best horse on the farms at his disposal. He was a good shot, and Chenalls was his guide to the best shooting-grounds. He sometimes fished, and Chenalls knew exactly where the choicest trout and the richest salmon were to be found. In fact, Chenalls entered so fully into the tastes of the young man, that Walter found him absolutely necessary to him to secure the enjoyments of a country life.

Having established this close intimacy, Chenalls never lost an opportunity of talking with Walter respecting Selina Penna. He soon satisfied himself that Walter, like most other young men who had led a dissipated life, had but a very low estimate of women generally. Acting upon this, he at first insinuated that Selina's innocence was but a mask, and at length he boldly assured Walter that the cottage girl was to be won by him with a few words, and that then he might put her aside at any time as a prize to some low-born peasant. Chenalls never failed to impress on Walter the necessity of keeping his uncle in the most perfect darkness, and of blinding the eyes of Selina's parents. Penna was, so thought Chenalls, easily managed, but there was more to be feared from the wife. Walter, however, with much artifice, having introduced himself to Honour Penna, employed the magic of that flattery, which, being properly applied, seldom fails to work its way to the heart of a weak-minded woman. He became an especial favourite with Honour, and the blinded mother was ever pleased at the attention bestowed with so little assumption, as she thought, of pride, on her daughter, by one so much above them.

Walter eventually succeeded in separating occasionally, though not often, Penna and his daughter. The witching whispers of unholy love were poured into the trusting ear. Guileless herself, this child-woman suspected no guile in others, least of all in one whom she had been taught to look upon as a superior being to herself. Amongst the villagers, the constant attention of Walter Trewoofe was the subject of gossip, and many an old proverb was quoted by the elder women, ill-naturedly, and implying that evil must come of this intimacy. Tom Chenalls was now employed by Walter to contrive some means by which he could remove Penna for a period from home. He was not long in doing this. He lent every power of his wicked nature to aid the evil designs of the young soldier, and thus he brought about that separation of father and child which ended in her ruin.

Near the Land's End the squire possessed some farms, and one of them was reported to be in such a state of extreme neglect, through the drunkenness and consequent idleness of the tenant, that Chenalls soon obtained permission to take the farm from this occupier, which he did in the most unscrupulous disregard for law or right. It was then suggested that the only plan by which a desirable occupier could be found would be to get the farm and farm-buildings into good condition, and that Penna, of all men, would be the man to bring this quickly about. The squire was pleased with the plan. Penna was sent for by him, and was proud of the confidence which his master reposed in him. There was some sorrow on his leaving home. He subsequently said that he had had many warnings not to go, but he felt that he dared not disoblige a master who had trusted him so far, so he went.

Walter needed not any urging on the part of Chenalls, though he was always ready to apply the spur when there was the least evidence of the sense of right asserting itself in the young man's bosom. Week after week passed on. Walter had rendered himself a necessity to Selina. Without her admirer the world was cold and colourless. With him all was sunshine and glowing tints.

Three months passed thus away, and during that period it had only been possible for Penna to visit his home twice. The father felt that something like a spirit of evil stood between him and his daughter. There was no outward evidence of any change, but there was an inward sense undefined, yet deeply felt like an overpowering fear that some wrong had been done. On parting, Penna silently but earnestly prayed that the deep dread might be removed from his mind.

There was an aged fisherman, who resided in a small cottage built on the sands, who possessed all the superstitions of his class. This old man had formed a father's liking for the simple-hearted maiden, and he had persuaded himself that there really was some foundation for the tales which the gossips told. To the fisherman, Walter Trewoofe was an evil genius. He declared that no good ever came to him, if he met Walter when he was about to go to sea. With this feeling he curiously watched the young man and maiden, and he, in after days, stated his conviction that he had seen 'merry maidens' rising from the depth of the waters, and floating under the billows, to watch Selina and her lover. He has also been heard to say, that on more than one occasion Walter himself had been terrified by sights and sounds. Certain, however, it is, these were insufficient, and the might of evil passions were more powerful than any of the protecting influences of the unseen world.

Another three months had gone by, and Walter Trewoofe had disappeared from Perranzabuloe. He had launched into the gay world of the metropolis, and rarely, if ever, dreamed of the deep sorrow which was weighing down the heart he had betrayed. Penna returned home – his task was done – and Chenalls had no reason for keeping him any longer from his wife and daughter. Clouds gathered slowly but unremittingly around him. His daughter retired into herself, no longer as of old reposing her whole soul on her father's heart. His wife was somewhat changed too – she had some secret in her heart which she feared to tell. The home he had left was not the home to which he had returned.

It soon became evident that some shock had shaken the delicate frame of his daughter. She pined rapidly; and Penna was awakened to a knowledge of the cause by the rude rejoicing of Chenalls, who declared that 'all people who kept themselves so much above other people were sure to be pulled down.' On one occasion he so far tempted Penna with sneers, at his having hoped to secure the young squire for a son-in-law, that the long-enduring man broke forth and administered a severe blow upon his tormentor. This was duly reported to the squire, and added thereto was a magnified story of a trap which had been set by the Pennas to catch young Walter; it was represented that even now they intended to press their claims, on account of grievous wrongs upon them, whereas it could be proved that Walter was guiltless – that he was indeed the innocent victim of designing people, who thought to make money out of their assumed misfortune. The squire made his inquiries, and there were not a few who eagerly seized the opportunity to gain the friendship of Chenalls by representing this family to have been hypocrites of the deepest dye; and the poor girl especially was now loaded with a weight of iniquities of which she had no knowledge. All this ended in the dismissal of Penna from the Squire's service, and in his being deprived of the cottage in which he had taken so much pride. Although thrown out upon the world a disgraced man, Penna faced his difficulties manfully. He cast off, as it were, the primitive simplicity of his character, and evidently worked with a firm resolve to beat down his sorrows.

He was too good a workman to remain long unemployed; and although his new home was not his happy home as of old, there was no repining heard from his lips. Weaker and weaker grew Selina, and it soon became evident to all, that if she came from a spirit-world, to a spirit-world she must soon return. Grief filled the hearts of her parents – it prostrated her mother, but the effects of severe labour, and the efforts of a settled mind, appeared to tranquillise the breast of her father. Time passed on, the wounds of the soul grew deeper, and there lay, on a low bed, from which she had not strength to move, the fragile form of youth with the countenance of age. The body was almost powerless, but there beamed from the eye the evidences of a spirit getting free from the chains of clay.

The dying girl was sensible of the presence of creations other than mortal, and with these she appeared to hold converse, and to derive solace from the communion. Penna and his wife alternately watched through the night hours by the side of their loved child, and anxiously did they mark the moment when the tide turned, in the full belief that she would be taken from them when the waters of the ocean began to recede from the shore. Thus days passed on, and eventually the sunlight of a summer morning shone in through the small window of this humble cottage, on a dead mother and a living babe.

The dead was buried in the churchyard on the sands, and the living went on their ways, some rejoicingly and some in sorrow.

Once more Walter Trewoofe appeared in Perran-on-the-sands. Penna would have sacrificed him to his hatred; he emphatically protested that he had lived only to do so; but the good priest of the Oratory contrived to lay the devil who had possession, and to convince Penna that the Lord would, in His own good time, and in His own way, avenge the bitter wrong.

Tom Chenalls had his hour of triumph; but from the day on which Selina died everything went wrong. The crops failed, the cattle died, hay-stacks and corn-ricks caught fire, cows slipped their calves, horses fell lame, or stumbled and broke their knees, a succession of evils steadily pursued him.

Trials find but a short resting-place with the good; they may be bowed to the earth with the weight of a sudden sorrow, but they look to heaven, and their elasticity is restored. The evil-minded are crushed at once, and grovel on the ground in irremediable misery. That Chenalls fled to drink in his troubles appeared but the natural result to a man of his character. This unfitted him for his duties, and he was eventually dismissed from his situation.

Notwithstanding that the Squire refused to listen to the appeals in favour of Chenalls, which were urged upon him by Walter, and that indeed he forbade his nephew to countenance 'the scoundrel' in any way, Walter still continued his friend. By his means Tom Chenalls secured a small cottage on the cliff, and around it a little cultivated ground, the produce of which was his only visible means of support. That lonely cottage was the scene, however, of drunken carousals, and there the vicious young men, and the no less vicious young women, of the district, went after nightfall, and kept 'high carnival' of sin. Walter Trewoofe came frequently amongst them; and as his purse usually defrayed the costs of a debauch, he was regarded by all with especial favour.

One midnight, Walter, who had been dancing and drinking for some hours, left the cottage wearied with his excesses, and although not drunk, he was much excited with wine. His pathway lay along the edge of the cliffs, amidst bushes of furze and heath, and through several irregular, zigzag ways. There were lateral paths striking off from one side of the main path, and leading down to the sea-shore. Although it was moonlight, without being actually aware of the error, Walter wandered into one of those, and before he was awake to his mistake, he found himself on the sands. He cursed his stupidity, and, uttering a blasphemous oath, he turned to retrace his steps.

The most exquisite music which ever flowed from human lips fell on his ear; he paused to listen, and collecting his unbalanced thoughts, he discovered that it was the voice of a woman singing a melancholy dirge:

The stars are beautiful, when bright
  They are mirror'd in the sea;
But they are pale beside that light
  Which was so beautiful to me.
My angel child, my earth-born girl,
  From all your kindred riven,
By the base deeds of a selfish churl,
  And to a sand-grave driven!
How shall I win thee back to ocean?
  How canst thou quit thy grave,
To share again the sweet emotion
  Of gliding through the wave?

Walter, led by the melancholy song, advanced slowly along the sands. He discovered that the sweet, soft sounds proceeded from the other side of a mass of rocks, which project far out over the sands, and that now, at low-water, there was no difficulty in walking around it. Without hesitation he did so, and he beheld, sitting at the mouth of a cavern, one of the most beautiful women he had ever seen. She continued her song, looking upwards to the stars, not appearing to notice the intrusion of a stranger.

Walter stopped, and gazed on the lovely image before him with admiration and wonder, mingled with something of terror. He dared not speak but fixed, as if by magic, he stood gazing on. After a few minutes, the maiden, suddenly perceiving that a man was near her, uttered a piercing shriek, and made as if to fly into the cavern. Walter sprang forward and seized her by the arm, exclaiming, 'Not yet, my pretty maiden, not yet.'

She stood still in the position of flight, with one arm behind her, grasped by Walter, and turning round her head, her dark eyes beamed with unnatural lustre upon him. Impressionable he had ever been, but never had he experienced anything so entrancing, and at the same time so painful, as that gaze. It was Selina's face looking lovingly upon him, but it seemed to possess some new power, a might of mind from which he felt it was impossible for him to escape. Walter slackened his hold, and slowly allowed the arm to fall from his hand. The maiden turned fully round upon him. 'Go!' she said. He could not move.

'Go, man!' she repeated. He was powerless.

'Go to the grave where the sinless one sleepeth!

Bring her cold corse where her guarding one weepeth;
Look on her, love her again, ay! betray her,
And wreath with false smiles the pale face of her slayer!
Go, go! now, and feel the full force of my sorrow!
For the glut of my vengeance there cometh a morrow.'

Walter was statue-like, and he awoke from this trance-like state only when the waves washed his feet, and he became aware that now it was only by wading through the waters that he could return around the point of rocks. He was alone. He called; no one answered. He sought wildly, as far as he now dared, amidst the rocks, but the lovely woman was nowhere to be discovered.

There was no real danger on such a night as this; therefore Walter walked fearlessly through the gentle waves, and recovered the pathway up from the sands. More than once he thought he heard a rejoicing laugh, which was echoed in the rocks, but no one was to be seen.

Walter reached his home and bed, but he found no sleep; and in the morning he arose with a sense of wretchedness which was entirely new to him. He feared to make any one of his rough companions a confidant, although he felt this would have relieved his heart. He therefore nursed the wound which he now felt, until a bitter remorse clouded his existence.

After some days, he was impelled to visit the grave of the lost one, and in the fulness of the most selfish sorrow, he sat on the sands and shed tears. The priest of the Oratory observed him, and knowing Walter Trewoofe, hesitated not to inquire into his cause of sorrow. His heart was opened to the holy man, and the strange tale was told – the only result being, that the priest felt satisfied it was but a vivid dream, which had resulted from a brain over-excited by drink. He, however, counselled the young man, giving him some religious instruction, and dismissed him with his blessing. There was relief in this. For some days Walter did not venture to visit his old haunt, the cottage of Chenalls. Since he could not be lost to his companions without greatly curtailing their vicious enjoyments, he was hunted up by Chenalls, and again enticed within the circle. His absence was explained on the plea of illness. Walter was, however, an altered man; there was not the same boisterous hilarity as formerly. He no longer abandoned himself without restraint to the enjoyments of the time. If he ever, led on by his thoughtless and rough-natured friends, assumed for a moment his usual mirth, it was checked by some invisible power. On such occasions he would turn deadly pale, look anxiously around, and fall back, as if ready to faint, on the nearest seat. Under these influences, he lost health.

His uncle, who was really attached to his nephew, although he regretted his dissolute conduct, became now seriously alarmed. Physicians were consulted in vain; the young man pined, and the old gossips came to the conclusion that Walter Trewoofe was ill-wished, and there was a general feeling that Penna or his wife was at the bottom of it. Walter, living really on one idea, and that one the beautiful face which was, and yet was not, that of Selina, resolved again to explore the spot on which he had met this strange being, of whom nothing could be learned by any of the covert inquiries he made.

He lingered long ere he could resolve on the task; but wearied, worn by the oppression of one undefined idea, in which, an intensity of love was mixed with a shuddering fear, he at last gathered sufficient courage to seize an opportunity for again going to the cavern.

On this occasion, there being no moon, the night was dark, but the stars shone brightly from a sky, cloudless, save a dark mist which hung heavily over the western horizon. Every spot of ground being familiar to him, who, boy and man, had traced it over many times, the partial darkness presented no difficulty.

Walter had scarcely reached the level sands, which were left hard by the retiring tide, than he heard again the same magical voice as before. But now the song was a joyous one, the burthen of it being:

Join all hands
  Might and main,
Weave the sands,
  Form a chain,
He, my lover,
  Comes again!

He could not entirely dissuade himself but that he heard this repeated by many voices; but he put the thought aside, referring it, as well he might, to the numerous echoes from the cavernous openings in the cliffs. He reached the eastern side of the dark mass of rocks, from the point of which the tide was slowly subsiding. The song had ceased, and a low moaning sound – the soughing of the wind – passed along the shore. Walter trembled with fear, and was on the point of returning when a most flute-like murmur rose from the other side of the rocky barrier, which was presently moulded into words:

From your couch of glistering pearl,
  Slowly, softly, come away;
Our sweet earth-child, lovely girl,
  Died this day, died this day.

Memory told Walter that truly was it the anniversary of Selina Pennaluna's death, and to him every gentle wave falling on the shore sung, or murmured 'Died this day, died this day.'

The sand was left dry around the point of the rocks, and Walter impelled by a power which he could not control, walked onward. The moment he appeared on the western side of the rock, a wild laugh burst into the air, as if from the deep cavern before him, at the entrance of which sat the same beautiful being whom he had formerly met. There was now an expression of rare joy on her face, her eyes glistened with delight, and she extended her arms, as if to welcome him.

'Was it ever your wont to move so slowly towards your loved one?'

Walter heard it was Selina's voice. He saw it was Selina's features; but he was conscious it was not Selina's form.

'Come, sit beside me, Walter, and let us talk of love.' He sat down without a word, and looked into the maiden's face with a vacant expression of fondness. Presently she placed her hand upon his heart; a shudder passed through his frame; but having passed, he felt no more pain, but a rare intensity of delight. The maiden wreathed her arm around his neck, drew Walter towards her, and then he remembered how often he had acted thus towards Selina. She bent over him and looked into his eyes. In his mind's mirror he saw himself looking thus into the eyes of his betrayed one.

'You loved her once?' said the maiden.

'I did indeed,' answered Walter, with a sigh.

'As you loved her, so I love you,' said the maiden, with a smile which shot like a poisoned dart through Walter's heart. She lifted the young man's head lovingly between her hands, and bending over him, pressed her lips upon and kissed his forehead, Walter curiously felt that although he was the kissed, yet that he was the kisser.

'Kisses,' she said, 'are as true at sea as they are false on land. You men kiss the earth-born maidens to betray them. The kiss of a sea-child is the seal of constancy. You are mine till death.'

'Death!' almost shrieked Walter.

A full consciousness of his situation now broke upon Walter. He had heard the tales of the gossips respecting the mermaid origin of Selina; but he had laughed at them as an idle fancy. He now felt they were true. For hours Walter was compelled to sit by the side of his beautiful tormentor, every word of assumed love and rapture being a torture of the most exquisite kind to him. He could not escape from the arms which were wound around him. He saw the tide rising rapidly. He heard the deep voice of the winds coming over the sea from the far west. He saw that which appeared at first as a dark mist, shape itself into a dense black mass of cloud, and rise rapidly over the star-bedecked space above him. He saw by the brilliant edge of light which occasionally fringed the clouds that they were deeply charged with thunder. There was something sublime in the steady motion of the storm; and now the roll of the waves, which had been disturbed in the Atlantic, reached our shores, and the breakers fell thunderingly within a few feet of Walter and his companion. Paroxysms of terror shook him, and with each convulsion he felt himself grasped with still more ardour, and pressed so closely to the maiden's bosom, that he heard her heart dancing of joy. At length his terrors gave birth to words, and he implored her to let him go.

'The kiss of the sea-child is the seal of constancy.'

Walter vehemently implored forgiveness. He confessed his deep iniquity. He promised a life of penitence.

'Give me back the dead,' said the maiden bitterly, and she planted another kiss, which seemed to pierce his brain by its coldness, upon his forehead.

The waves rolled around the rock on which they sat; they washed their seat. Walter was still in the female's grasp, and she lifted him to a higher ledge. The storm approached. Lightnings struck down from the heavens into the sands, and thunders roared along the iron cliffs. The mighty waves grew yet more rash, and washed up to this strange pair, who now sat on the highest pinnacle of the pile of rocks. Walter's terrors nearly overcame him; but he was roused by a liquid stream of fire, which positively hissed by him, followed immediately by a crash of thunder, which shook the solid earth. Tom Chenall's cottage on the cliff burst into a blaze, and Walter saw, from his place amidst the raging waters, a crowd of male and female roisterers rush terrified out upon the heath, to be driven back by the pelting storm. The climax of horrors appeared to surround Walter. He longed to end it in death, but he could not die. His senses were quickened. He saw his wicked companion and evil adviser struck to the ground, a blasted heap of ashes, by a lightning stroke, and at the same moment he and his companion were borne off the rock on the top of a mountainous wave, on which he floated; the woman holding him by the hair of his head, and singing in a rejoicing voice, which was like a silver bell heard amidst the deep base bellowings of the storm:

Come away, come away,
  O'er the waters wild!
  Our earth-born child
Died this day, died this day.

Come away, come away!
  The tempest loud
  Weaves the shroud
For him who did betray.

Come away, come away!
  Beneath the wave
  Lieth the grave
Of him we slay, him we slay.

Come away, come away!
  He shall not rest
  In earth's own breast
For many a day, many a day.

Come away, come away!
  By billows tost
  From coast to coast,
  Like deserted boat
  His corse shall float
Around the bay, around the bay.

Myriads of voices on that wretched night were heard amidst the roar of the storm. The waves were seen covered with a multitudinous host, who were tossing from one to the other the dying Walter Trewoofe, whose false heart thus endured the vengeance of the mermaid, who had, in the fondness of her soul, made the innocent child of humble parents the child of her adoption.